YOUR KNOWLEDGE HAS VALUE

Philipp Rott

Behaviorism - a short discussion

GRIN Verlag

Bibliografische Information der Deutschen Nationalbibliothek:

Die Deutsche Bibliothek verzeichnet diese Publikation in der Deutschen National-
bibliografie; detaillierte bibliografische Daten sind im Internet über http://dnb.d-
nb.de/ abrufbar.

Imprint:

Copyright © 2000 GRIN Verlag GmbH
Druck und Bindung: Books on Demand GmbH, Norderstedt Germany
ISBN: 978-3-656-52953-8

This book at GRIN:

http://www.grin.com/en/e-book/45359/behaviorism-a-short-discussion

„Behaviorism"
Psycholinguistics
SS 2000

1 Introduction

How do children learn to speak? And why? Do all children start to use language at some age? Or do they need a certain "trigger"? Is our ability to use a language innate? Or are we conditioned to use language as a response to our environment? There are many other questions to be raised, for example about the function of a language, the process of acquisition, or the meaning of the term "language" as such. Psycholinguistics tries to answer at least some of these questions.

> "Psycholinguistics is the name given to the study of the psychological processes involved in language. Psycholinguists study understanding, producing, and remembering language. […][They are] concerned with listening, reading, speaking, writing, and memory for language […] [and] interested in how we acquire language, and the way in which it interacts with other psychological systems." (Harley, 1995: p.1)

Thus, psycholinguistics is concerned with "(…) the correlation between linguistic behaviour and psychological processes thought to underlie that behaviour (…)" (Crystal, 1992: p. 291).

Due to its interdisciplinary nature, psycholinguistics has been influenced both by linguistic and psychological findings and theories. One of the main psychological schools which have contributed to psycholinguistic theories is behaviourism. Although early behaviourism was not concerned with language as such, but rather with the observation of any (animal or human) behaviour, Burrhus Frederic Skinner (1904-1990) later focussed his interest on verbal behaviour. He employed behaviouristic methods and tried to describe the acquisition process as a complex form of conditioning. One of his aims was to apply his findings in the development of new teaching methods.

This paper is designed to give a brief overview on behaviouristic key terms and ideas. Due to its importance for psycholinguistic aspects, the main focus will be on Skinner's behaviourism, although the "roots" of behaviourism will also be mentioned shortly. The concluding part of this paper deals with Skinner's theories on verbal behaviour and the controversy they aroused. Some of the most common critical remarks concerning Skinner's ideas will be presented and commented upon.

2 Early Behaviourism

In 1913, John Broadus Watson published a provocative paper about psychology in which he argued that psychology should not waste its time being concerned with introspection, the observation of one's inner processes, but it should rather study publicly observable behaviour, i. e. behaviour which can be observed by other persons as well. (see Zimbardo, 1995: p. 9) Watson stated that a science had to be founded on observable data, not on speculations about what is going on in a person's mind, which behaviourists call the "black box".

In his work, Watson was largely influenced by the findings of Russian physiologist Ivan Pavlov and his classical conditioning. Pavlov had discovered that a physiological response, such as salivation, could be triggered by stimuli which originally were not thought to elicit this reaction, for example the ringing of a bell. (ibd.) In Pavlov's experiments with dogs, the neutral stimulus (the bell) was constantly followed by the unconditioned stimulus (food), which then caused the unconditioned response (salivation). After some "training", the dogs produced saliva on hearing the bell ring, although they had not been offered food. The neutral stimulus had become a conditioned stimulus and the unconditioned response had turned into a conditioned response.

Watson concluded that every human behaviour was based on this kind of inborn or conditioned sequence of stimulus and response and claimed that, therefore, introspection was unnecessary as both stimuli and responses were potentially observable data. He thought that every behaviour was a response to some environmental stimulus, and, thus, it was possible to predict the response or behaviour of a person whenever a certain stimulus was given. Likewise, he considered it possible to say what kind of stimulus had elicited a given response.

Watson's aim was to predict and to control human behaviour. He thought that "(…) if all behaviour could be shown to be the result of learning, it would open up new possibilities for changing undesirable behaviour." (Zimbardo, 1995: p.10) This idea about the possibility of controlling human behaviour on the one hand and his devotion to observable data and the rejection of introspection on the other hand were the main features that distinguished behaviourism from all other psychological schools at that time.

3 The Formative Period

As has been mentioned before, psycholinguistics is an interdisciplinary field of study and, thus, depends on the prevailing theories of both psychology and linguistics. In the 1950s, a period which is also called the Formative Period, Structuralism, which was the prevailing paradigm in linguistics at that time, as well as behaviourism were interested in deriving theoretical constructs from observable data by using a set of verifiable operations which are highly explicit. (see Kess, 1992: 14 ff)

Behaviourism "(…) attempted to make psychology into a rigorous science – every bit as rigorous as the established sciences like physics and chemistry (…)" (Cattell, 2000: p.32) and allowed only "(…) evidence that could be publicly inspected, was open to scrutiny by other scientists, and was therefore considered to be objective (…)." (ibd.)

Likewise, structural linguistics was concerned with describing, observing and analysing language. Generalisations about the structure of a language, according to structuralists, could only be based on objectively and systematically observed data. (see Aitchison, 1995:p.24) The study of meaning and of psychological factors involved in language did not suffice for these demands and, thus, were not dealt with by structuralists.

While behaviourists were convinced that it was possible to predict human behaviour, Bloomfield, who was the first linguist to promote the demands for rigorous and systematical analysis in linguistics and who can be said to have been the most important figure in descriptive linguistics (or strucuralism), was rather aware of the complexity of the matter. He claimed that, although he thought it possible in principle, to predict people's actions (i.e. also verbal behaviour), it would be necessary to know the exact structure of the body at the given point in time, its structure at birth and any stimulus that had ever affected the organism. (see Bloomfield, 1933: p. 33 in: Cattell, 2000: p.36)

However, F. B. Skinner, the radical behaviourist, took an opposing view in his work on "Verbal Behaviour" and tried to describe and analyse the complex relationship between environmental factors in the verbal community and the actual verbal responses they cause. Skinner's radical behaviourism, his method of operant conditioning and, particularly, his ideas about verbal behaviour have had a major influence on psycholinguistic views and language acquisition theories and, thus, also on teaching methods.

4 Skinner's Behaviourism

One of the most ardent followers of behaviouristic priciples, Frederic Burrhus Skinner (1904-1990) was fascinated by the works and ideas of Watson and Pavlov. Nevertheless, his theories and interests are to be distinguished from the work they conducted. "It is not unusual to read or hear comments that equate Skinner's and Pavlov's interests. However, they are very different. The work for which Pavlov is famous concentrated on the study of relatively simple, reflexive-type responses." (Nye, 1992: p. 13) Skinner did not study these kinds of reflexive-type behaviour, but concentrated on "(…)what commonly are considered to be 'voluntary' behaviours." (Nye, 1992: p.14) His focus was not on "elicited" responses, but on "emitted" behaviours, their effects and the environmental conditions. (see ibd.) He called these "emitted responses" (that were both *caused by* and in turn *had some effect on* the surrounding) *operants* and, thus, his form of conditioning came to be called *operant conditioning.*

> "An operant is any behaviour that is emitted by an organism and can be characterised in terms of the observable effects it has on the environment. Literally, operant means affecting the environment, or operating on it (…)." (Zimbardo, 1995: p. 258)

Responses that have the same effect, but vary slightly in their form, belong to the same class of operant behaviour.

4.1 Operant Conditioning

The main difference between Skinnerian operant conditioning and the (classical) conditioning of Pavlov is that in operant conditioning "(…) a response must be emitted before it can be reinforced." (Nye, 1992: p.14) While Pavlov was concerned with (reflexive-type) responses that were conditioned to occur on a stimulus which would not normally trigger this kind of response, Skinner analysed the circumstances under which a certain behaviour would occur, the behaviour itself and the consequences of that behaviour. (ibd.) Just as Pavlov had done, he used animals to conduct his experiments. He tested them in an apparatus commonly known as the "Skinner box", which allowed the experimenter to create specific conditions, to keep down the number of potentially interfering influences and to measure and record the results.

Pavlov had manipulated the stimuli which preceded the response; Skinner, however, manipulated the consequences a certain (operant) behaviour had. The result was that the probability of a certain behaviour decreased or increased. "Operant conditioning, then, modifies the probability of different types of operant behaviour as a function of the environmental consequences they produce." (Zimbardo, 1995: p. 258)

With the help of his operant chamber (Skinner box), Skinner tested rats and other animals, and measured their "learning progress" by the increasing or decreasing frequency of a response. For example, if a rat had been offered food every time it had pressed a lever, and this led to more frequent pressing of the lever by the rat, Skinner interpreted this as "learning". The constant offering of food as the consequence of the rat's behaviour, thus, reinforced this kind of behaviour. "Significant events that can strengthen an organism's responses if they are contingently related are called reinforcers." (Zimbardo, 1995: p. 259)

Just as the offering of food (positive reinforcer) increased the rat's pressing the lever, an aversive stimulus might increase the frequency or probability of a certain response, if this response results in the removing of the aversive stimulus. In positive reinforcement, then, the subject is rewarded for a certain kind of behaviour (which will then occur more frequently); in negative reinforcement the subject will also show a given behaviour more frequently, only this time does the subject *not* obtain a reward, but it avoids an aversive stimulus. (see Zimbardo, 1995: p. 259)

A way of decreasing the frequency of a given behaviour is to withhold the delivery of the positive reinforcer. "If the behaviour does not produce any consequences, it returns to the level it was before operant conditioning – in other words, it is extinguished." (Zimbardo, 1995: p. 259) This kind of decreasing the frequency of a behaviour is called operant extinction.

Punishment is another way of decreasing the frequency of a given response, but it works rather differently. "A punisher is any stimulus that – when it is made contingent upon a response – decreases the probability of that response over time." (Zimbardo, 1995: p. 260) For example, the hangover after a long night in the pubs might result in less frequent (excessive) consumption of alcohol.

Skinner claimed that, by the techniques used in operant conditioning, every kind of human behaviour might be manipulated and controlled. His animals were, indeed, trained to perform rather "unusual" actions, such as playing table-tennis. Also, some of his techniques have been applied more or less successfully in education, industry, business, government, prisons, mental institutions and family settings. (see Nye, 1992: p. 15) Nevertheless, his attempt to explain the process of language acquisition in terms of the model of operant conditioning led to some controversy among linguists.

4.2 Verbal Behaviour

Skinner's suggestion was that verbal behaviour, like other forms of behaviour was the result of a complex form of conditioning. The human species, according to Skinner, underwent a "unique evolutionary change when its vocal musculature came under operant control and when vocal behavior began to be shaped and maintained by its reinforcing consequences" (Skinner, 1990a : p. 1206 in: Nye, 1992: p.33). The process of shaping, then, plays an important role in language acquisition:

> "Utterances that vaguely resemble words are given attention and praise at first, and then progressively improving performance is required for further reinforcement. In this way the child's verbal behaviour is *shaped* until the language can be spoken in an acceptable way." (Nye, 1992: p.33)

As with other forms of behaviour, Skinner argues that verbal behaviour has consequences on the environment, i.e. the verbal community. These consequences serve as stimuli (reinforcers) for the verbal behaviour.

The development of verbal behaviour, thus, can only be explained if we know "the conditions under which it was acquired (…)" (Skinner, 1974: p. 100) and if we can answer the

7

following questions: "What speech has the child heard? Under what circumstances has he heard it? What effects has he achieved when he has uttered similar responses?" (ibd.) In other words, we need to know all about the verbal behaviour itself, about the environmental factors potentially having effect on a response and we need to know the effects of the given verbal behaviour itself to see which consequences result in an increased frequency of the verbal behaviour (i.e. serve as reinforcers) and which do not.

Skinner's attempt was to find out more about the environmental factors, or as he called them "external variables" (Skinner, 1953: p.35 in: Nye, 1992: p. 43), which affected behaviour. He considered the relationship between external variables and verbal behaviour to be a functional relationship and, therefore, referred to his interpretation of verbal behaviour as a "functional analysis". (see Nye, 1992: p.43)

Skinner's analysis and interpretation of verbal behaviour comprised many different and complex aspects of language, not all of which can be related to here. Much against the common presumption that Skinner did not care to analyse creative or abstract use of language (e.g. metaphors), some of his ideas and writings reveal his eagerness to explain these complexities of language use. At this point, however, only the basic forms verbal behaviour can take can be explained.

Skinner differentiated between several forms of verbal behaviour (verbal operants) that have distinct effects and are part of an individual's verbal repertoire. Mands, for example, "occur under conditions of deprivation or aversive stimulation and basically take the form of commands or demands. They are unusual (…) in that they *specify* their reinforcing consequences." (Nye, 1992: p.44) A person who has not had anything to eat for some time may say "Give me something to eat", and the command will be reinforced if he is actually given food as a result of it . Somebody who is being tickled may say "Stop it" and will receive reinforcement if the addressed person actually stops tickling him or her. These kinds of verbal operants are already conditioned in early development of a child's verbal behaviour.(ibd.)

Another form of verbal operants are the *tacts*, which simply refer to and name objects, events and their properties. (ibd.) For example, a person may see a well-staged play and say to his neighbour: "What a great performance!" The discriminative stimulus in this case would of course be the play, or rather the properties of the play, and the reinforcer might be the neighbour's consent (either spoken, for example "It surely is", or non-verbal, such as nodding). While mands already specify what kind of response would be reinforcing, tacts can be reinforced by a variety of consequences. (ibd.)

Another important aspect of Skinner's theory is the fact that

"Apart from an occasional relevant audience, verbal behavior requires
no environmental support. (…) As a result, verbal behavior can occur
on almost any occasion. (…) [One] important consequence is that the
speaker also becomes a listener and may richly reinforce his own
behavior." (Skinner, 1974: pp. 89,90)

As Nye (1992) puts it, "in part, "thinking" consists of our continuous reactions to, and
revisions of, our own verbal behaviour." (p. 44) The verbal community influences the way a
person behaves verbally, i.e. speaks, but the resulting verbal behaviour can be shown (or *not
shown*, as in thinking) at almost any time.

5 Controversy

Skinner's views have certainly been most controversial among both psychologists and
linguists. His ideas have often been misunderstood or misinterpreted. His suggestion that by
controlling our environment we should control behaviour to improve our society is, in itself,
most controversial and has been the root of heated arguments about his original aims ever
since. Furthermore, many people were appalled by the idea that, basically, human behaviour
works in the same way as animal behaviour does. However, as these are rather ethical
concerns, not specifically related to the subject of language acquisition, they shall not be
considered here (though their importance for other fields of studies or general ethical issues
cannot be neglected).

With regard to the concept of shaping applied to the development of verbal behaviour, one
might suggest that, according to Skinner, children learn a language only by imitating what
they hear (the environmental circumstances of their behaviour) and if every single utterance is
constantly   reinforced. Skinner rather considered language to be made up of "units" which
can be composed into new combinations. (see Harris & Coltheart, 1986: p. 31) Creative use of
language is therefore, according to Skinner, not only possible; it is, in fact, the result of the
complex procedures of shaping and chaining, it is due to a "history of reinforcement" (see
Nye, 1992: p.72) "As with other behaviors, Skinner suggested that creativity is the result of a
person's genetic endowment and environmental experiences." (ibd.) (This suggestion already
refutes the following points of criticism concerning Skinner's alleged denial of innate factors
in language acquisition.)

Many critics have challenged Skinner's views claiming that the theory does not account
for innate factors affecting the development of language abilities (Nye, 1992: p.44). As with

"emotions", these factors are inaccessible to scientific investigation and are, thus, not taken into consideration. According to these critics, Skinner denies any speculations about what is going on in the "black box" and demands empirical analysis of behaviour rather than introspection, but he does not provide this empirical framework for the analysis of linguistic material and "rests entirely on speculative extension of his experimental analysis of animal behaviour" (de Cecco, 1969: p.308). Yet Skinner does not say that "Verbal Behaviour" is the result of experimental work. On the contrary, he explicitly states that "the emphasis is not upon experimental or statistical facts, the book is not theoretical in the usual sense." (Skinner, 1957: p.12 in: De Cecco, 1969: p. 325) Skinner simply attempts to apply behaviouristic principles to verbal behaviour (see Richelle, 1993: p. 123): "The present extension to verbal behavior is thus an exercise in interpretation rather than a quantitative extrapolation of rigorous experimental results." (Skinner, 1957: p. 12 in : De Cecco, 1969: p. 325)

Similarly, Skinner does not deny the possibility of innate factors affecting language acquisition. He simply wants to *focus* on the outward (observable) factors that influence language use, not on the genetic, innate factors. He says, "It may be true that there is no structure without construction, but we must look to the constructing environment, not to a constructing mind." (Skinner, 1974: p. 117)

Among others, Noam Chomsky was, of course, the "leading figue" in criticising Skinner. The result of his devastating criticism was

> "that the questions raised by Skinner, which are crucial issues in the psychology of language, though possibly not in linguistics, were totally overlooked for more than a decade, as long as Chomsky's formalistic views dominated the field." (Richelle, 1993: p. 120)

Skinner may have neglected some aspects of language acquisition which appear to be important in order to come to a conclusive theory. However, it seems that many critics were so appalled by Skinner's visions of "controlling" behaviour that they did not consider the fruitful aspects of his work that are still relevant in psychology, linguistics and psycholinguistics as well as in educational and teaching programmes.

6 Summary

Although behaviouristic principles and ideas have largely contributed to the development of psychological and psycholinguistic theories, they have been met controversially ever since their emergence in the early twentieth century. Skinner, in particular, was criticised strongly for basing his work solely on animal experiments and transferring the outcome of these experiments to such complex phenomenons as language acquisition. Moreover, his critics claimed that his work neglected the influence of innate factors on language acquisition. Nevertheless, some of his basic concepts, particularly operant conditioning, have proved to be of certain value for the analysis of human behaviour as such, and, to some extent, for the difficult task of developing a comprehensive theory concerning language acquisition. However, it seems obvious that Skinner's "Verbal Behaviour", though providing some interesting and fruitful ideas, cannot explain the entire process of language acquisition.

7 Literature

- Aitchison, Jean: **Linguistics. An Introduction.** London : Hodder and Stoughton, 1995.

- Bloomfield, Leonard: **Language.** New York: Holt, Rinehart and Winston, 1933.

- Cattell, Ray: **Children's Language. Consensus and Controversy.** London: Cassell, 2000.

- De Cecco, John P.: **The Psychology of Language, Thought, and Instruction: Readings.** London: Holt, Rinehart and Winston, 1969.

- Garnham, Alan: **Psycholinguistics : Central Topics.** London and New York: Methuen, 1985.

- Harley, Trevor A.: **The Psychology of Language. From Data to Theory.** Hove: Psychology Press Ltd., 1995.

- Harris, Margaret and Max Coltheart: **Language Processing in Children and Adults. An Introduction.** London/New York: Routledge and Kegan, 1986.

- Kess, Joseph F.: **Psycholinguistics : Psychology, Lingustics, and the study of natural language.** Amsterdam: John Benjamins, 1992.

- Nye, Robert D.: **The legacy of B. F. Skinner : Concepts and Perspectives, Controversies and Misunderstandings.** Pacific Grove, Calif. : Brooks/Cole, 1992.

- Nye, Robert D.: **What is B. F. Skinner really saying?** Englewood Cliffs, N.J. : Prentice-Hall, 1979.

- Richelle, Marc: **B. F. Skinner : A Reappraisal.** Hove and Hillsdale : Erlbaum, 1993.

- Skinner, Burrhus F.: **About Behaviorism.** London : Cape, 1974.

- Skinner, Burrhus F.: **Can Psychology be a science of the mind?** in: *American Psychologist*, Vol. 45, No. 11, 1990, pp. 1206-1210.

- Skinner, Burrhus F.: **Science and Human Behavior.** New York: Macmillan, 1953.

- Skinner, Burrhus F.: **The Behavior of Organisms.** New York: Appleton-Century-Crofts, 1938.

- Skinner, Burrhus F.: **Verbal Behavior.** New York: Appleton-Century-Crofts, 1957.

- Zimbardo, Philip G.: **Psychology : A European Text.** London : Harper Collins, 1995.